Collins
MUSIC

GREAT
Body Percussion Songs

TOPICAL SONGS FOR SCHOOLS

CD/CD-ROM
NO MUSIC READING REQUIRED
WHITEBOARD POPUPS
AND FULL AUDIO SUPPORT

Compiled and arranged
by Steve Grocott

Performed by Rosemary Amoani,
Dominic Stitchbury, Cleveland Watkiss
and Steve Grocott

Introduction

Making vocal sounds and body percussion is surely the oldest form of human communication and music making. It is from these starting points that we developed the languages and music we have today. Each of us completes the same journey from babbling and banging as babies to speaking, singing and clapping.

All around the world different cultures have developed their body percussion specialities from the flamenco clapping of Spain to the solkattu vocal rhythms of India. There is even armpit music from Ethiopia.

Two of the most famous music educators, Orff and Kodaly, both made extensive use of body percussion. Orff is particularly strong on the deep connection between language and rhythm.

The songs and arrangements in this collection are starting points for exploration. They are necessarily simple so that everyone can be included but this does not mean that the experts should be held back. Many children will already be highly skilled in, for example, playground clapping games or beatboxing.

The movements of body percussion shade inevitably into dance. This is wonderful for involving the whole of ourselves in the music and for generating a sense of group togetherness ~ so important in the wellbeing of the class.

A little attention to technique brings huge benefits in performance. Familiar sounds like clapping can be very much improved simply by giving attention to the sound you are making. It is easy to make three distinct clapping sounds: a bass sound with hollow hands, an alto sound like normal applause and a higher sound with flattened hands. Having different sounds means you can start to build patterns.

New sounds can be found if we are prepared to experiment and don't focus only on the louder ones. All sorts of pops, scrapes, taps and squeaks will emerge. When we include vocal sounds in the mix the sonic pallet is virtually limitless. Many of these sounds are funny ~ raspberries are inevitable. As teachers, we have to be prepared for a certain amount of hilarity and disorder before we get the genie back in the bottle and start making the sounds work in musical arrangements.

The web is an endless source of ideas and inspiration. Just put 'Body percussion', 'How to make a finger pop sound' or 'Hambone' into your search engine. Two good sites for seeing what is possible and how it's done are 'Tribal Groove' and 'Body Rhythm Factory'.

My hope is that you will use a mix and match approach, applying the techniques and ideas in these songs to all kinds of other material. I know that if you do, you and your children will have a lot of fun and so will your audience.

Steve Grocott

WHAT'S YOUR BEAT?

INTRODUCTION (spoken)

Click (click)
Clap (clap)
Flippety flap (flippety flap)
Stamp! (stamp)

VERSE (sung)

Click clap flippety flap,
Stamp your feet, (stamp)
Flippety flap click clap,
What's your beat?

BODY PERCUSSION JAM

▶ **CD track 1** (performance) **track 2** (backing)
track 3 (teaching)
▶ **CD-ROM**: audio-embedded lyrics/melody; movie;
lesson plan; piano accompaniment

SHOW ME ONE CLICK

Show me one click (click) one click,
Show me one clap (clap) one clap,
Show me one stamp (stamp) one stamp,
Now let's see if we can do some more.

Show me two clicks (click, click) two clicks,
Show me two claps (clap, clap) two claps,
Show me two stamps (stamp, stamp) two stamps,
Now let's see if we can do some more.

Show me three clicks (click, click, click) three clicks…

Show me four clicks (click, click, click, click) four clicks…

Show me five clicks (click, click, click, click, click) five clicks…

Show me six clicks (click, click, click, click, click, click) six clicks,
Show me six claps (clap, clap, clap, clap, clap, clap) six claps,
Show me six stamps (stamp, stamp, stamp, stamp, stamp, stamp) six stamps,
I don't think that we can do anymore

▶ CD track 4 (performance) track 5 (backing) track 6 (teaching) track 7 (backing/faster)
track 8 (performance/faster) track 9 (Show me one sound/performance/faster)
▶ CD-ROM: audio-embedded lyrics/melody; slide show; lesson plan; piano accompaniment

Introduction

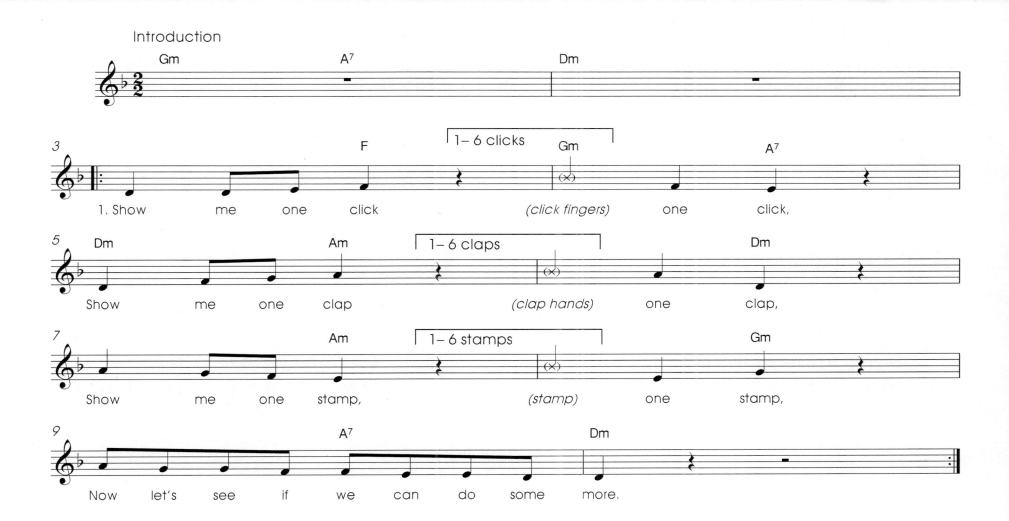

MIX IT UP

Listen up ~ listen up listen up,
Can you hear me now? ~ listen up listen up,
Here comes the kick ~ listen up listen up,
   b b b b   b b b b
Can you hear me now ~ listen up listen up,
Here comes the rim shot,
   k k k k   k k k k

    Come on everybody listen up,
    Come on everyone gonna mix it up.
b k b k k b k b k k

      CHORUS
     Come on everybody, listen up,
     Come on everyone, gonna mix it up,
     Everybody, let's have a party,
     Bass is thumping, everybody jumping
       on the floor.
      b k b k k b k b k k

Listen up ~ listen up listen up,
Can you hear me now? ~ listen up listen up,
Closed high hat ~ listen up listen up,
   ts ts ts ts   ts ts ts ts
Can you hear me now ~ listen up listen up,
Open high hat,
   tsss tsss   tsss tsss   tsss tsss   tsss tsss

    Come on everybody listen up,
    Come on everyone gonna mix it up.
ts tsss   ts tsss   ts ts tsss ts tsss

      CHORUS
     Come on everybody, listen up,
     Come on everyone, gonna mix it up,
     Everybody, let's have a party,
     Bass is thumping, everybody jumping
       on the floor.
      ts tsss   ts tsss   ts ts tsss ts tsss

▶ **CD** track 10 (performance) track 11 (backing) track 12 (teaching)
▶ **CD-ROM**: audio-embedded lyrics/melody; movies; lesson plan; piano accompaniment

Listen up ~ listen up listen up,
Can you hear me now? ~ listen up listen up,
Mixing it up ~ listen up listen up,
   b   k   ts tsss   b   k   ts tsss
Can you hear me now ~ listen up listen up,
Mixing it up,
   b   k   ts tsss   b   k   ts tsss
   Come on everybody listen up,
   Come on everyone gonna mix it up.
   b   k   ts tsss   b   k   ts tsss

   CHORUS
   Come on everybody, listen up,
   Come on everyone, gonna mix it up,
   Everybody, let's have a party,
   Bass is thumping, everybody jumping
   on the floor.
   b   k   ts tsss   b   k   ts tsss

Listen up ~ listen up listen up,
Can you hear me now? ~ listen up listen up,
Making it up ~ listen up listen up,
   (beatbox freestyle)
Can you hear me now? ~ listen up listen up,
Making it up,
   (beatbox freestyle)
   Come on everybody listen up,
   Come on everyone gonna mix it up.
   (beatbox freestyle)

   CHORUS
   Come on everybody, listen up,
   Come on everyone, gonna mix it up,
   Everybody, let's have a party,
   Bass is thumping, everybody jumping
   on the floor.
   (beatbox freestyle)

Listen up, listen up, listen up,

1 2 3 4 ~ listen up!

MIX IT UP • (continued)

MIX IT UP by Steve Grocott • *Great Body Percussion Songs* • © 2011 HarperCollins*Publishers* Ltd. • www.collins.co.uk

LATE FOR SCHOOL

Foot-clap click-click now, foot-clap click-click,
Foot-clap click-click now, foot-clap click-click,
Foot-clap click-click now, foot-clap click-click,
Foot-clap click-click now, foot-clap click-click.

Right hand clap and a left hand clap,
Right hand clap and a left hand clap,
Right hand clap and a left hand clap,
Right hand clap and a left hand clap.

CHORUS
  Clap clap pitta pat pitta pat pitta pat,
  Clap clap pitta pat pitta pat pitta pat,
  Clap clap pitta pat pitta pat pitta pat,
  Clap clap pitta pat pitta pat clap clap.

I'm late for school, now I'm late for school,
I broke the rule, now I look a fool,
I'm late for school, now I'm late for school,
I broke the rule, now I look a fool.

Woke up late ~ half past eight,
Want my breakfast and it's getting late,
Dog ate the toast ~ cat stole the fish,
Baby put the milk in the butter dish.

  Clap clap pitta pat pitta pat pitta pat…

I'm late for school, now I'm late for school,
I broke the rule, now I look a fool,
I'm late for school, now I'm late for school,
I broke the rule, now I look a fool.

Now I'm late ~ teacher at the gate,
I'll never get a sticker if I make her wait,
Half past nine ~ never on time,
Friends in class, I'm the last in line.

  Clap clap pitta pat pitta pat pitta pat…

FIRST SECTION OF VERSE ~ stamp, clap, fingerclick fingerclick × 2 each line:
SECOND SECTION OF VERSE~ slap right thigh, clap, slap left thigh, clap
CHORUS ~ clap, then hands sweep thighs twice for each pitta pat

► **CD** track 13 (performance) **track 14** (backing) **track 15** (teaching)
► **CD-ROM:** audio-embedded lyrics/melody; movie; lesson plan; piano accompaniment

KAERU • FROG SONG

SAMPLE INTRODUCTION AND OSTINATO ACCOMPANIMENT (CROAKED)

Gwa gwa, gwa gwa, gero gero gero gero, gwa gwa gwa.

UNISON SONG

Kaeru no uta ga,
Kikoete kuru yo,
Gwa gwa gwa gwa,
Gero gero gero gero gwa gwa gwa.

ROUND

GROUP 1 Kaeru no uta ga, Kikoete kuru yo…

GROUP 2 Kaeru no uta ga, Kikoete kuru yo…

SAMPLE CODA (CROAKED)

Gwa gwa, gwa gwa.

POND MUSIC (VOCAL IMPROVISATION)

▶ **CD** track 16 (performance) track 17 (backing) track 18 (teaching)
▶ **CD-ROM**: audio-embedded lyrics/melody; slide show; movie;
lesson plan; piano accompaniment

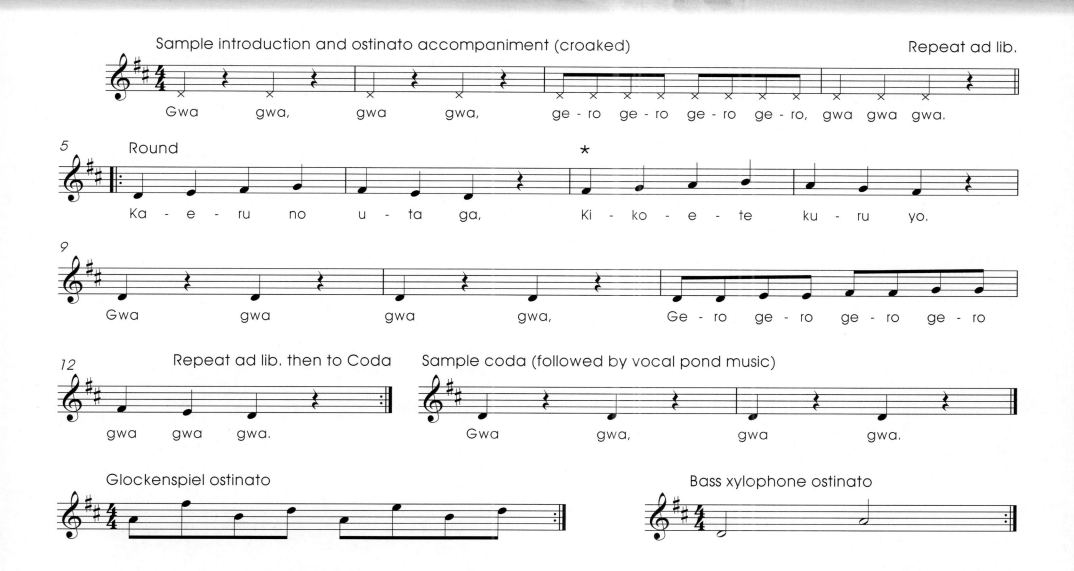

* **round entry point**

MISS MARY MAC

CALL

Miss Mary Mac,
All dressed in black,
With silver buttons,
All down her back,

She cannot read,
She cannot write,
But she can smoke,
Her father's pipe,

She asked her mother,
For fifty pence,
To see the elephants,
Jump over the fence,

They jumped so high,
They reached the sky,
And they never came back,
'Till the 4th of July,

She went up stairs,
And banged her head,
And now she's dead!

RESPONSE

Mac Mac,
black black,
buttons buttons,
back back.

read read,
write write,
cough cough,
ugh yuck!

mother mother,
pence pence,
elephants elephants,
fence fence.

high high,
sky sky,
back back,
July July.

oh dear,
oh no,

CALL

Dum dum dum dum ~
Dum dum dum dum ~
Dum dum dum dum ~
Dum dum dum dum …

Repeat for length of song then sing from the beginning again:

Miss Mary Mac, Mac Mac…

JAMMING SOLO

(improvise body percussion)

knees	clap	knees	clap	knees	clap	knees	clap

Miss Mary   Mac,   Mac,   Mac, All dressed…

▶ **CD** track 19 (performance) **track 20** (backing) **track 21** (teaching)
▶ **CD-ROM**: audio-embedded lyrics/melody; slide show; movie; lesson plan; piano accompaniment

Acknowledgements

The author and publishers would like to thank Ian Russell and Margaret Omoniyi two wonderful music teachers who tested the material with their pupils and gave invaluable feedback. Thanks also to Dominic Stitchbury for beatboxing advice.

What's your beat, **Show me one click**, **Mix it up**, **Late for School** by Steve Grocott, © 2011 Steve Grocott. Copyright administered by HarperCollins*Publishers* Ltd. All rights reserved.

Kaeru, **Miss Mary Mac**, arranged from traditional by Steve Grocott, © 2011 Steve Grocott. Copyright administered by HarperCollins*Publishers* Ltd. All rights reserved.

Published by Collins
An imprint of HarperCollins*Publishers*
The News Building
1 London Bridge Street
London Bridge
SE1 9GF

HarperCollins*Publishers*
1st Floor Watermarque Building
Ringsend Road
Dublin 4
Ireland

www.collins.co.uk

© 2011 HarperCollins*Publishers* Ltd

ISBN 978-1-4081-4710-8

Printed and bound in Great Britain by Ashford Colour Press Ltd.

Text and music arrangements © 2011 Steve Grocott
Lesson plans by Maureen Hanke © HarperCollins*Publishers* Ltd.

Filming by Adrian Downie © HarperCollins*Publishers* Ltd.

Cover and inside images © Shutterstock Images LLC

Series edited and developed by Sheena Roberts

Designed by Saffron Stocker
Music setting by Jeanne Roberts
Sound engineering by Steve Grocott
Post production by Ian Shepherd, Mastering Media